RIFLE SQUAD AND PLATOON

in

ATTACK

ILLUSTRATED

By

MAJOR FRANK F. RATHBUN, Infantry

The Military Service Publishing Company
Harrisburg, Pennsylvania

Copyright June 1954 by

The Military Service Publishing Co.
Harrisburg, Pa.

First Edition, June 1954

ALL RIGHTS RESERVED

Library of Congress Catalog Card Number: 54-9067

Printed in the U.S.A.
By
The Telegraph Press
Established 1831
Harrisburg, Pa.

FOREWORD

There is no type of human endeavor where it is so important that those in authority possess basic and detailed knowledge of their job, as that of the profession of arms. The Army exists to win battles and in the final analysis this depends on small-unit commanders. Indirectly, it also means that commanders at the company, battalion, and regimental level must possess the know-how to see that squads and platoons are taught how to reach their objective with the minimum loss of life. This small volume is an excellent guide, not only for the leaders of the small units, but for those who would train them. Its careful study will answer the inevitable questions of what to do and how to convert decisions into practical maneuvers on the ground.

Every young man is surprised when he is first exposed to the violence of modern warfare. I am sure that more than one has had the thought, "So this is what it's like," flash through his mind and on taking stock of his reactions, has realized that—in spite of everything—he possesses the ability to think clearly and to act as he has been trained.

To be thus surprised at the intensity of enemy action is normal, but to permit small units to go into action without proper preparation is inexcusable. The commander who follows the guidance in this training document will never have cause to feel that men's lives entrusted to him have been lost because of faulty instruction, and the small-unit commander who masters the principles contained herein will never feel inadequate on the battlefield.

J. C. Fry

J. C. FRY
Major General USA
Chief, Career Management Division
Department of the Army

AUTHOR'S PREFACE

The young military leader, both commissioned and non-commissioned, is constantly faced with the problem of knowing how to use the tools of his trade. These tools, more often than not, are his men and weapons.

In combat and in peacetime tactical training, the most frequent question the junior leader asks himself is, "What do I do now?" I have seen units fail to take their objectives because their leaders could not answer this question promptly, or, more often, because they didn't have the **right** answer.

This book has been prepared to help the junior infantry leader. It tells him what to do, when to do it, and how to do it. An important phase of infantry small-unit tactics—the attack—is presented in a series of graphic illustrations and a few well-chosen words. The basic essentials are stressed in such a way that they are easy to read and easy to remember. The material is adapted from FM 7-10, "Rifle Company, Infantry Regiment," and reflects the latest tactical doctrine as it is being taught at The Infantry School.

This is a combat leader's book, written and illustrated in a clear-cut, down-to-earth style. It is a book for all junior military leaders and for all aspiring young men who hope someday to become leaders.

This book could not have been completed without the accomplished assistance of Mr. Charles Gonzales Rebeles, who prepared the illustrations. He combined his talent as an artist with his experience as a soldier to make the written portion of this book come to life.

Frank F. Rathbun

FRANK F. RATHBUN
Major, Infantry

The Infantry School
Fort Benning, Georgia
1 March 1954

CONTENTS

Chapter 1 — Page
The Attack in General 7

Chapter 2
Squad and Platoon Organization 17

Chapter 3
Combat Formations 23

Chapter 4
Getting the Platoon Ready for the Attack 33

Chapter 5
The Platoon in Attack 47

Chapter 6
The Rifle Squad in Attack 62

Chapter 7
The Weapons Squad in the Attack 82

Appendix I
Sample Platoon Leader's Order 90

Appendix II
Sample Squad Leader's Order 94

Index 96

CHAPTER 1

THE ATTACK IN GENERAL

Before we trace the step-by-step movement of the rifle squad and platoon through an attack—for that is what this book intends to do—let's look at our basic ideas on attack in general. These ideas are few and simple. But, knowing them, we can more quickly understand **how** the squad and platoon do their job. We can more readily see **why** these units are organized and armed as they are. And we can learn to plan for their use in a way that will make the most of their fighting abilities.

The Infantry's Job

The infantry's job in the attack is to kill or capture the enemy. We do this by **fire** and **maneuver**—which simply means that we use part of a force on the battlefield to pin the enemy down with fire while the rest moves in close to finish the job.

Fire Superiority

We believe that fire superiority over the enemy is the first and most important step in the attack. To whip the enemy and avoid friendly casualties, we plan to plaster him right from the beginning of a scrap and keep it up all the way through. We plan to hit him with so much fire that he can't get out of his holes to fight or fire back and can't use his own heavy fire against us to any great extent.

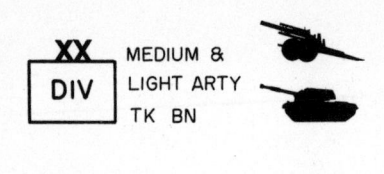

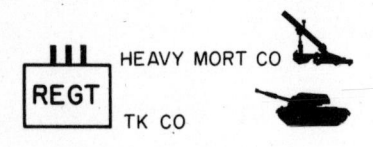

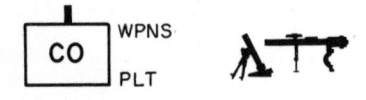

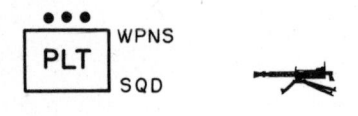

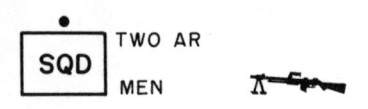

DIV (XX)	MEDIUM & LIGHT ARTY / TK BN
REGT (III)	HEAVY MORT CO / TK CO
BN (II)	HEAVY WPNS CO
CO (I)	WPNS PLT
PLT (•••)	WPNS SQD
SQD (•)	TWO AR MEN

Organization for Fire Support

The infantry division is organized from top to bottom to provide this fire support for its attacking units. Each of its major units—the division itself, the regiments, the battalions, the companies, and the platoons—has its own fire support unit. Even within the rifle squad are two automatic rifles that the squad leader uses to cover the movement of his men and to keep fire superiority over the enemy until the last shot is fired.

Maneuvering Force

Important as all this fire power is, we know that fire alone, no matter what kind or how heavy, cannot drive a determined enemy from his positions. He must be finished off by **close combat**—by men overrunning his position to kill or capture him.

This is the job of the **maneuvering** forces. Once again, infantry organization is built to order for the job at hand. Before an enemy can be licked, there are three steps that must be followed. These steps, which have been known for years in the infantry as the "Four F's," are these:

FIND'EM & FIX'EM

FIGHT'EM

FINISH'EM

Finding 'em

Finding an organized enemy is not as easy as it sounds. You may know that he occupies a certain hill or woods. But that's not enough. You need to know where he is strong, where he is weak, and where his weapons and flanks are.

Fixing 'em

Immediately after finding the enemy, you have to **fix 'em**—that is, hold them in position so that you can move in and hit them where it hurts the most. Fixing and finding are usually taken as parts of the same step, because as soon as you find the enemy, you must keep them from getting away or from changing position to meet your attack. This you do by placing all kinds of fire on and around their positions.

Fighting 'em

After you have found and fixed the enemy, you carry the fight to them, hitting them heaviest where they are least able to take the blow.

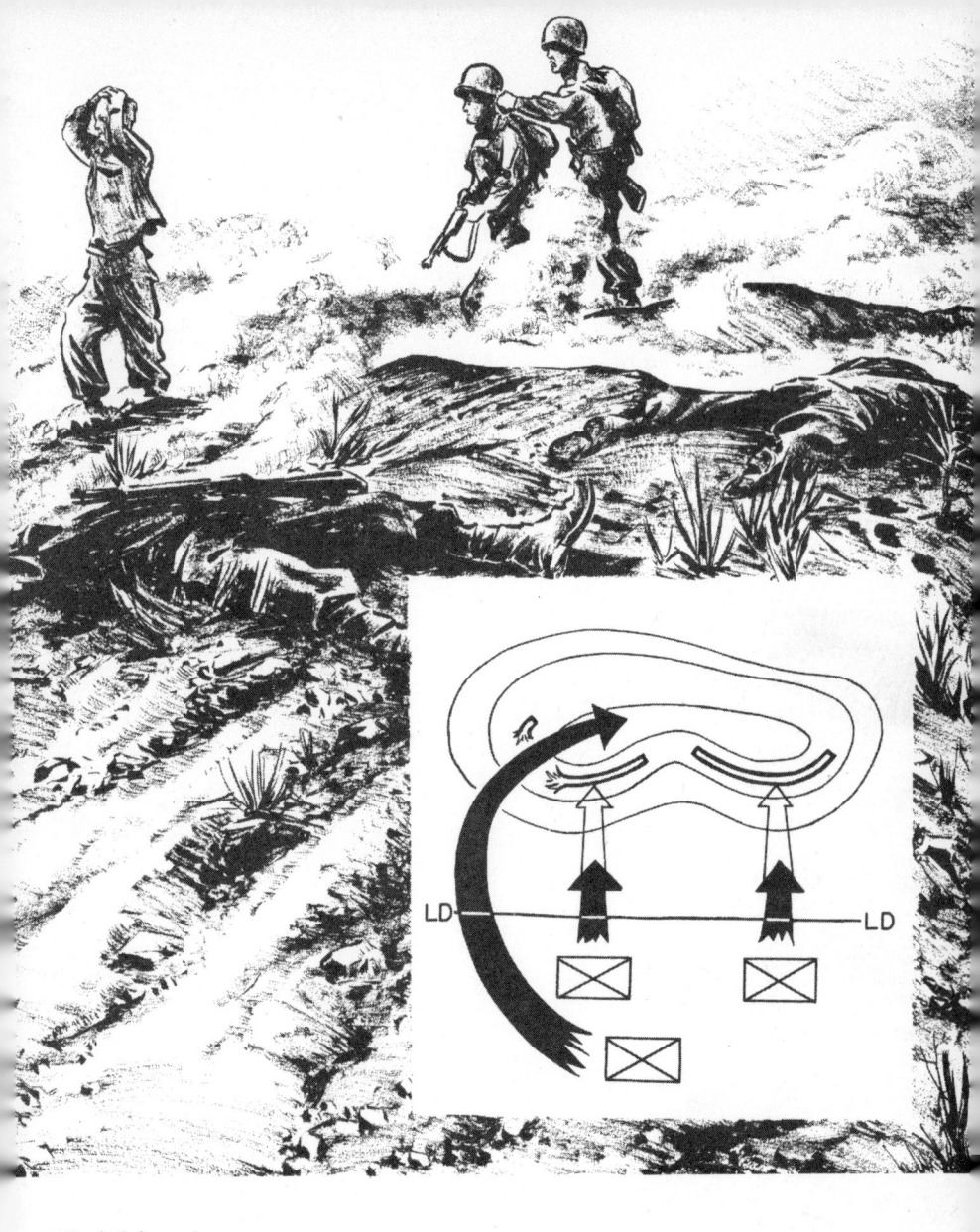

Finishing 'em

After you hit the enemy, you push right on, giving them no chance to recover. Your big job now is to use whatever strength is necessary to prevent their escape and to kill or capture them.

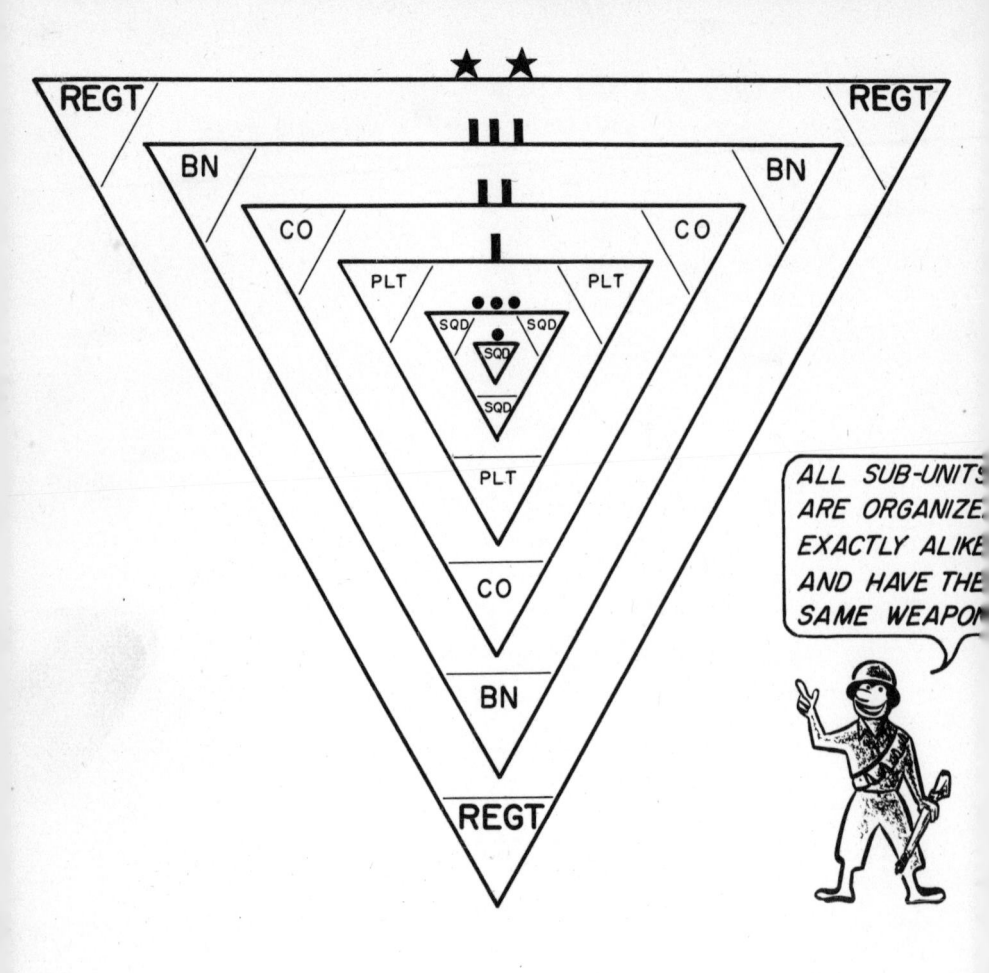

ALL SUB-UNITS ARE ORGANIZED EXACTLY ALIKE AND HAVE THE SAME WEAPONS

Triangular Infantry Organization

Infantry units are organized with these three steps —and fire support—in mind. Break down any infantry unit and you will find it is organized in "threes," giving us the so-called triangular organization. Two of these units are usually used to find, fix, and fight and the third to help finish.

CHAPTER 2
SQUAD AND PLATOON ORGANIZATION
The Rifle Squad

The rifle squad has nine members. For purposes of drill and assigning duties, the men are numbered.

1   2   3   4   5   6   7   8   9

The number 1 man is the squad leader and number 9 is the assistant squad leader. Both are armed with the M1 rifle and carry grenade launchers.

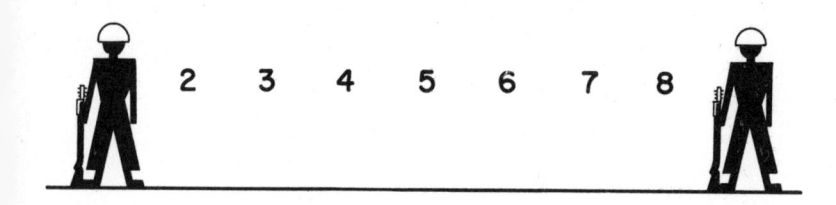

Numbers 2, 3, 4, 7, and 8 are all riflemen, but some of them have additional duties.

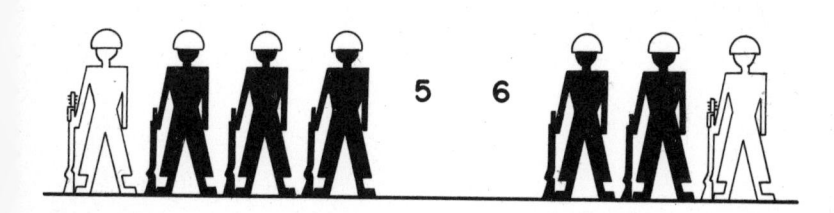

The number 3 man—the sniper—is armed with the M1C (sniper's) rifle. The number 4 man, armed with the M1, carries another grenade launcher. Numbers 7 and 8, armed with the M1, carry additional ammunition for the automatic riflemen.

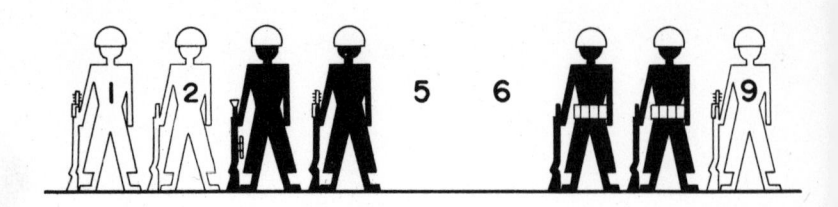

Numbers 5 and 6 are the automatic riflemen.

The Rifle Platoon

The rifle platoon is made up of three rifle squads, a weapons squad, and platoon headquarters—a total of 45 men who are trained to move and fight together.

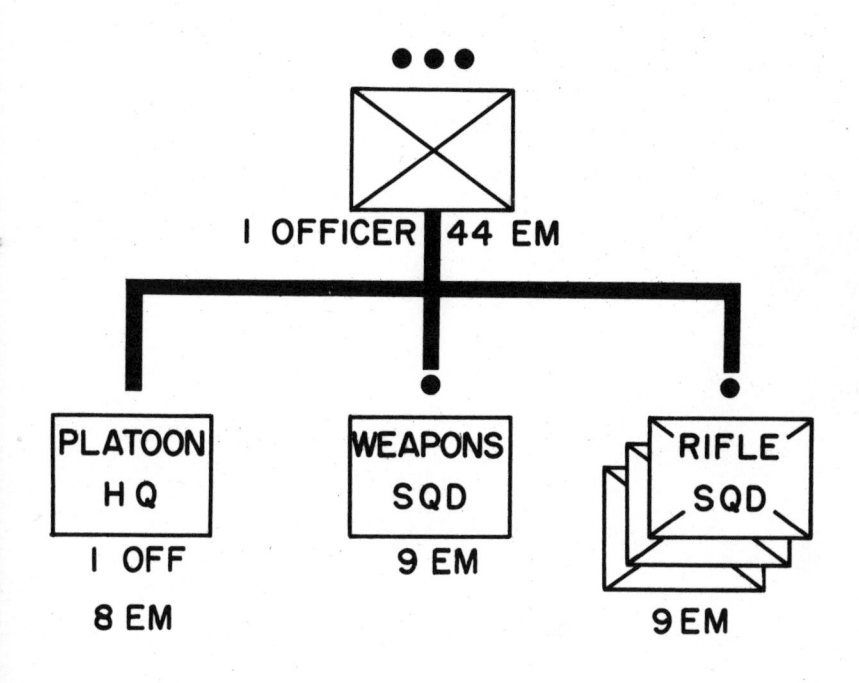

```
              • • •
          ┌─────────┐
          │  ╲   ╱  │
          │    ╳    │
          │  ╱   ╲  │
          └─────────┘
        I OFFICER  44 EM
      ┌───────┼───────┐
┌─────────┐ ┌─────────┐ ┌─────────┐
│ PLATOON │ │ WEAPONS │ │  RIFLE  │
│   HQ    │ │   SQD   │ │   SQD   │
└─────────┘ └─────────┘ └─────────┘
   I OFF       9 EM        9 EM
   8 EM
```

The rifle squads, all organized alike, are the maneuvering part of the platoon. The weapons squad, with its two light, air-cooled machine guns, is the fire support element.

Platoon Headquarters

Platoon headquarters, which commands and controls the unit, has nine men. The platoon leader—a first or second lieutenant—is armed with a carbine. He is responsible for the platoon's welfare, training, and leadership.

Helping him lead and control the platoon are his platoon sergeant and assistant platoon sergeant. The first one is a master sergeant, the second a sergeant first class. Both are armed with the M1 rifle.

The next two men are messengers. Both are privates first class, armed with the M1 rifle.

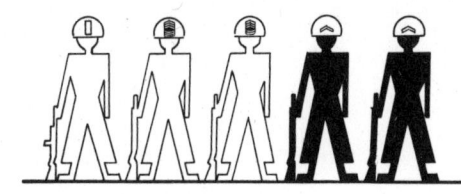

The last four men make up the rocket launcher team. This team's main job is to knock out enemy armor. The gunner and assistant gunner carry pistols. One of the ammunition bearers is armed with the M1 rifle, the other with a carbine. The gunner is a corporal, the rest of the men privates first class.

Weapons Squad

The weapons squad also has nine men. It is led by a sergeant first class, armed with an M1 rifle. The rest of the squad is made up of two four-man machine gun teams. There is no assistant squad leader.

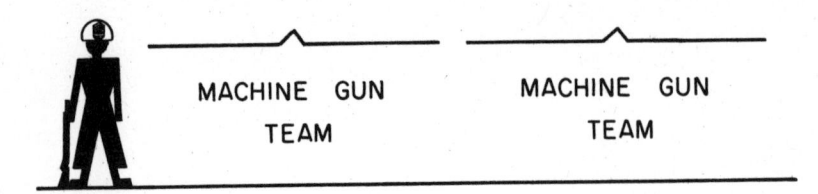

Each machine gun team has a corporal gunner, an assistant gunner, and two ammunition bearers. The gunners and assistant gunners carry pistols. One ammunition bearer in each team is armed with an M1 rifle, the other with a carbine. All men, except the gunner, are privates first class.

CHAPTER 3
COMBAT FORMATIONS

In the early days of infantry combat, close-order drill and the manual of arms formed the basis of combat formations. Units were massed for ease of control by their leaders and so they could deliver a heavy volume of fire and make a final bayonet charge together. Against modern artillery and automatic weapons, such formations would result in mass suicide.

Essentials of Combat Formations

Modern-day squads and platoons must be able to maneuver over all kinds of terrain in wide-open formations, often where the enemy can see them or where he has already planned heavy defensive fires. So, our combat formations must enable units to reach their objective **fast** and in shape to **fight as a team.**

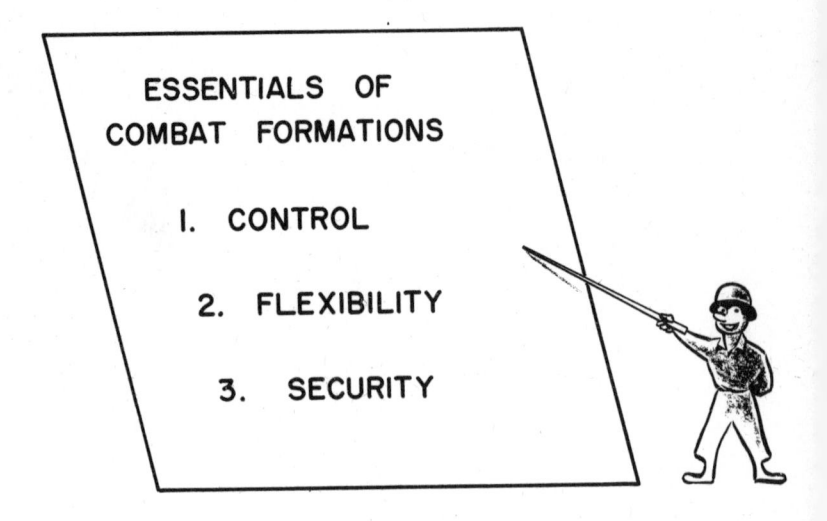

```
ESSENTIALS OF
COMBAT FORMATIONS

 1. CONTROL

 2. FLEXIBILITY

 3. SECURITY
```

To accomplish these things, there are three basic essentials for combat formations: **control** by leaders; **flexibility,** so we can shift from one formation to another; and **security** from enemy action.

SQUAD FORMATIONS: Squad Column

The first of three basic squad formations is the squad column. We use it when control and speed are most needed and when security is not too important. It is good for moving through woods, fog, smoke, or darkness, and when moving along trails and roads, or through defiles.

The squad column is flexible; you can move from it into either of the other formations. Its major weakness is the fact that it is wide open to automatic fire from the front and because the men in it cannot fire to the front without changing formation.

25

The Squad Diamond

The squad diamond keeps the squad from bunching up and gives good all-around security. The automatic riflemen on the flanks can fire to the front, flanks, or rear. The formation is easily controlled by the squad leader in open terrain. From this formation he can move quickly into **as skirmishers** for the assault.

Its main weakness is the fact that it is hard to control in rough or wooded terrain.

As Skirmishers

As skirmishers is usually used for the assault because it enables the squad to pour all of its fire to the front over a fairly wide area. It is also suitable for crossing small, open spaces or areas exposed to enemy observation.

Its main weakness is that it is hard to control. The squad leader and his assistant usually stay behind, one to each side, where they can best watch and direct the squad.

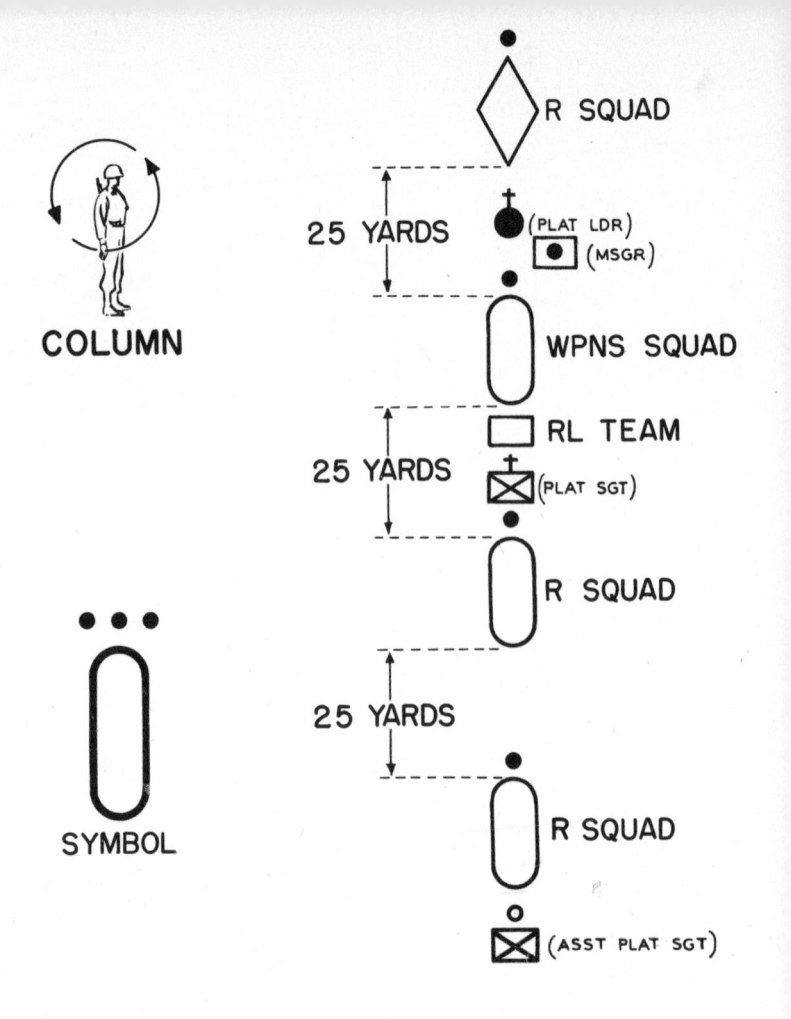

PLATOON FORMATIONS: Platoon Column

There are five basic platoon combat formations—the column, the wedge, the echelon, the vee, and the line.

The platoon column is used for the same purpose as the squad column. It is good for control and speed and it favors action to the flanks.

It is formed by the first squad, which is the base squad, moving in squad diamond, while the others follow in squad column.

```
                    R SQUAD
        40 YARDS


   R SQUAD      WPNS SQUAD      R SQUAD

                  RL TEAM


      WEDGE              SYMBOL
```

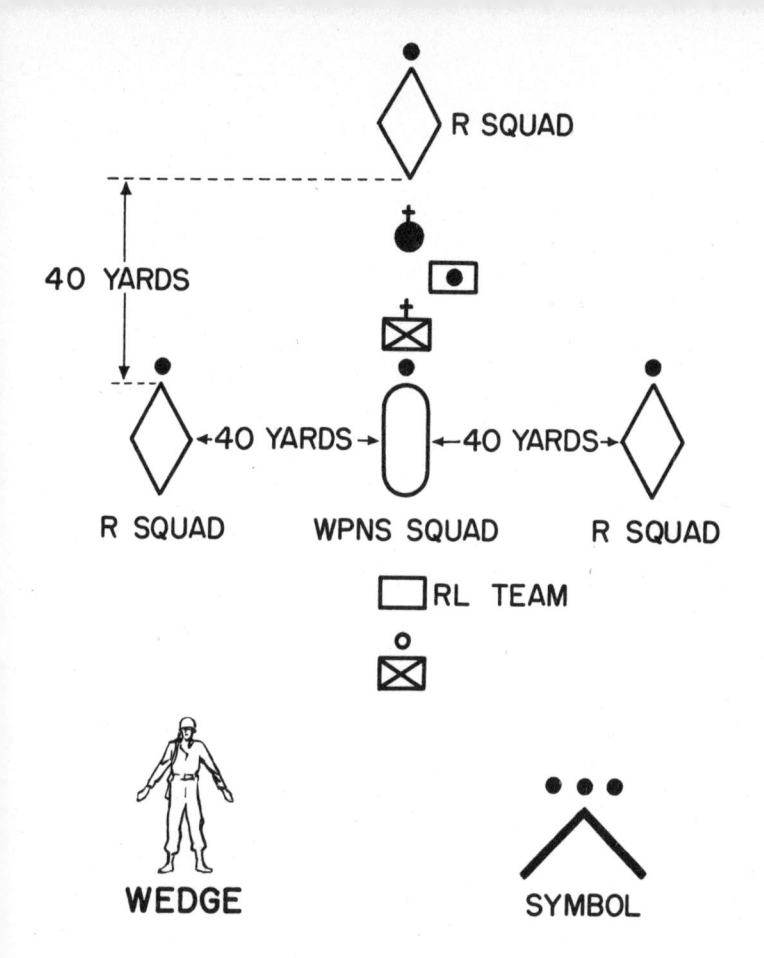

Platoon Wedge

To form the platoon wedge, the three rifle squads take up the diamond formation, with the number one squad in the lead. The weapons squad stays at the center in squad column, ready for quick movement wherever needed.

The wedge provides the best all-around security. It is particularly good when the men need to be spread out wide and when the platoon operates alone. The formation is not good when the terrain is too rough or wooded.

[Diagram: Platoon Echelon Right (Left) formation showing R Squad, WPNS Squad, RL Team positions with 40 YDS spacing, and symbols for LEFT and RIGHT echelon]

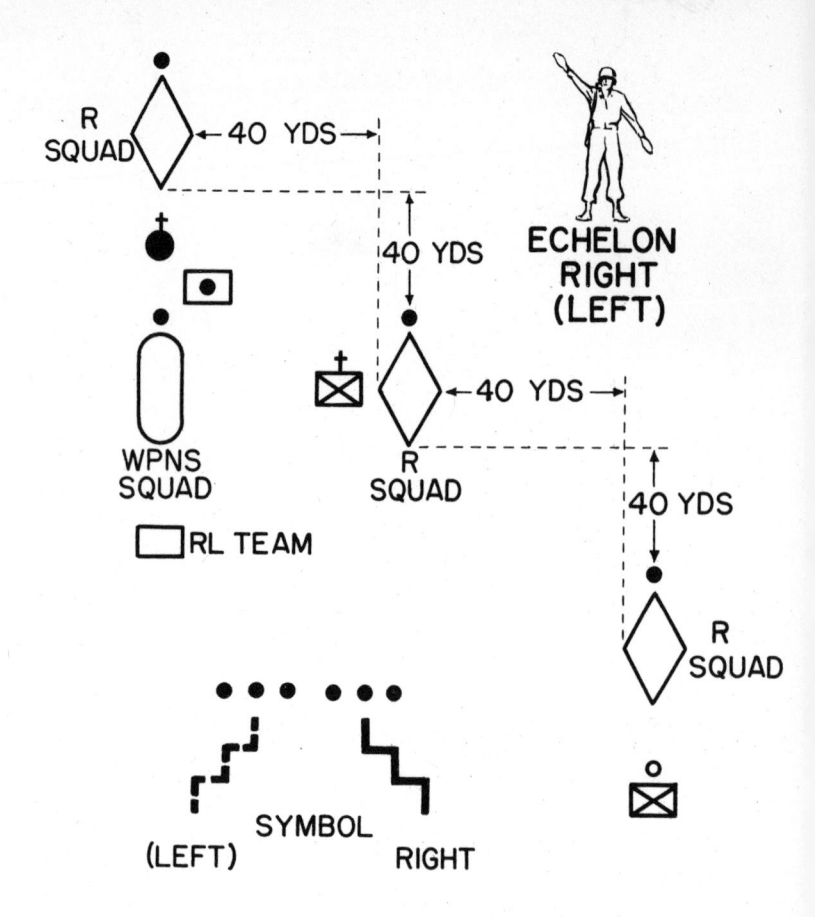

Platoon Echelon

The platoon echelon is generally used when the platoon is protecting an open flank of a large unit or when enemy action is expected from one of the flanks. It is made by the rifle squads, in diamond formation, forming to the side and rear of the base squad. The weapons squad, again in column, follows behind the base squad.

The echelon permits heavy fire to the front and in the direction of the guarded flank. It is hard to control and there must be good visibility between squads.

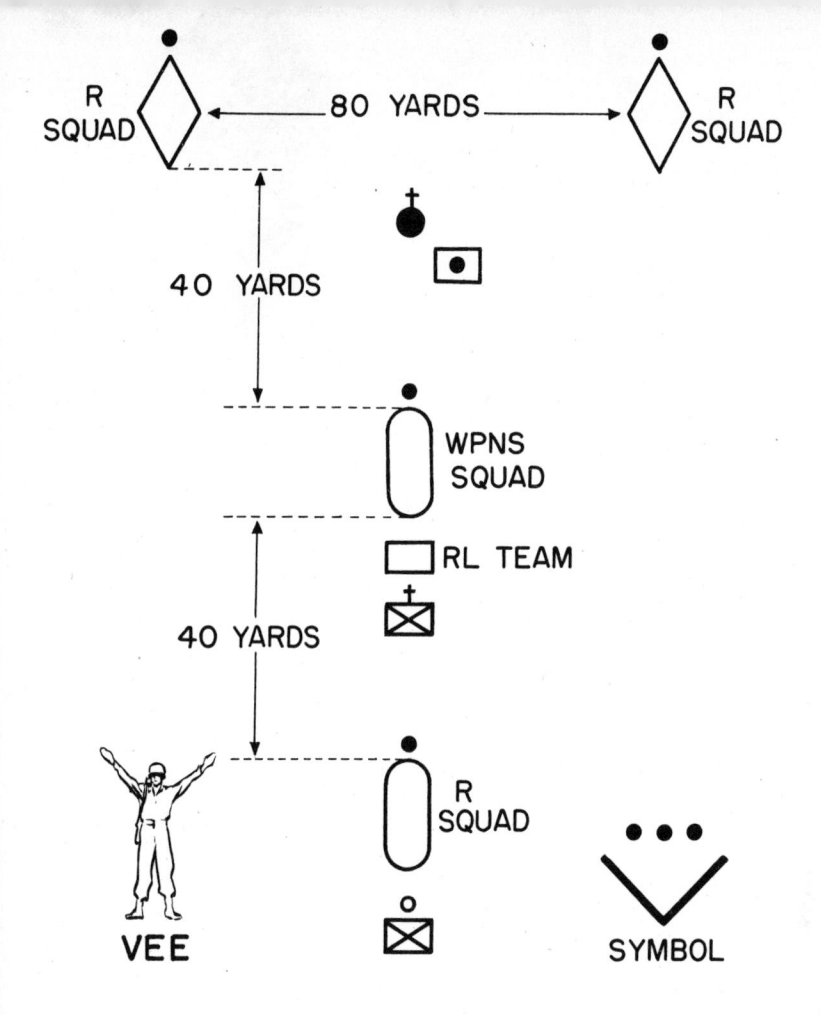

```
    R                                    R
  SQUAD  ◆ ←——— 80 YARDS ———→ ◆  SQUAD


              ↕
        40 YARDS
              ↕

                    WPNS
                    SQUAD

                  ☐ RL TEAM
                  ⊠
        40 YARDS
              ↕
                    R
                    SQUAD
                                      • • •
                  ⊠                    ╲╱
  VEE                                SYMBOL
```

Platoon Vee

The platoon vee has two rifle squads in diamond formation on a line, while the weapons squad and the third rifle squad follow in squad column.

The vee allows fair control by the platoon leader, is flexible, and provides good all-around security and dispersion. It is used against fairly well-known enemy resistance and to cross short, exposed areas. Like the wedge, it may not be usable in rough or wooded terrain.

```
    R              R              R
  SQUAD    40    SQUAD    40    SQUAD
    |←—  YDS  —→|←—  YDS  —→|
```

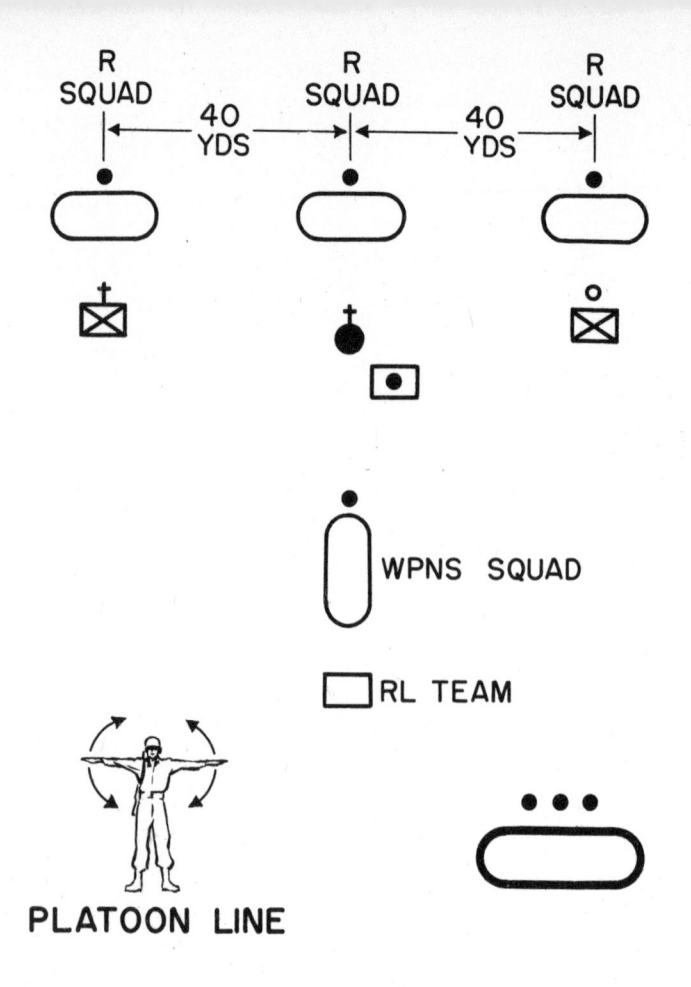

Platoon Line

  The platoon's assault formation is called the platoon line. Like the squad's "as skirmishers," it allows heavy fire to the front and covers a wide area. The platoon usually assaults with three squads abreast in **as skirmishers** formation.

  The platoon line may also be used for crossing short, open spaces under enemy observation. But it is not generally used for maneuver, other than the assault, because it does not provide good **control, flexibility,** and all-around **security**.

OBJECTIVE

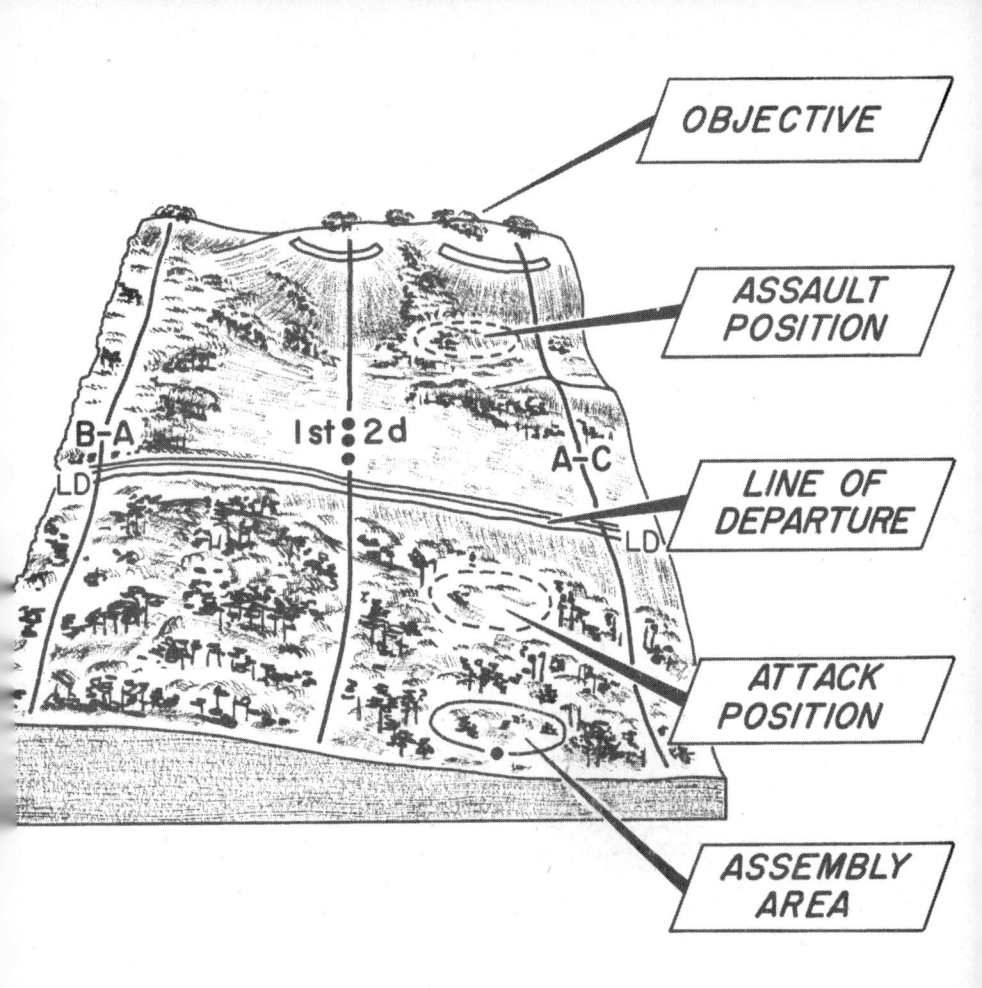

ASSAULT POSITION

LINE OF DEPARTURE

ATTACK POSITION

ASSEMBLY AREA

CHAPTER 4
GETTING THE PLATOON READY FOR THE ATTACK

The rifle platoon may be all or a part of the company's attacking force or of the reserve. It seldom fights alone. The platoon uses the fires of its own and attached weapons—as well as the bigger supporting weapons further back—to fix the enemy and move to a position from which it can rush in to kill or capture him.

The Company Attack Order

If possible, the company commander gives his attack order at or near his company observation post (OP). Or, he may take the platoon leaders to the OP for a quick look at the terrain, then give his order in a covered position farther back. He may have to rely on maps, rough terrain models, or sketches to describe the terrain.

The platoon leader usually takes his platoon sergeant and a messenger with him to get the company attack order.

Troop Leading Steps

After the platoon leader gets the company attack order, he has many things to do in a short time to make sure that his mission will succeed. The six troop leading steps that follow, either memorized or jotted in a notebook, will help him organize his thoughts and actions.

1. Begin planning
2. Make arrangements for:
   a. Movement of platoon
   b. Reconnaissance
   c. Coordination
3. Go on reconnaissance
4. Complete plan
5. Issue Order
6. Supervise

Beginning Planning

The platoon leader begins to plan as soon as he knows his platoon mission. He studies a map to see how the terrain can help or hinder him. He considers what the enemy can do to slow or stop him. He thinks of different courses of action to get his platoon on the objective. His plans, of course, include many details from the company order, such as objective, line of departure, attack position, time of attack, and supporting weapons.

Making Arrangements

The platoon leader sends a messenger back to the platoon with instructions for its movement. Then he plans his reconnaissance, deciding where he can go in the time left. He must allow time to complete his plan and issue his order, and still leave time for his squad leaders to go on reconnaissance, make plans, and issue orders. He decides when and where he will issue his order and sends a messenger back to have his squad leaders meet him.

TELL SGT. BAKER I WANT TO MEET THE SQUAD AND ROCKET TEAM LDRS. AT THE OP AT 0815 AND.....

Arranging Coordination

The platoon leader also arranges for coordination with unit leaders on his right and left to avoid any mix-ups. He coordinates with the weapons platoon leader for the reporting time and place for weapons squads attached to him and for close fire support from the platoon. He arranges to check his plan of attack with the company commander.

Going on Reconnaissance

On reconnaissance, the platoon leader is seeking ways to make the terrain work for him. He looks for: (1) **critical terrain features,** usually high ground that gives him an advantage over the enemy; (2) **observation** points that will help him control the platoon and **fields of fire** from both his own and the enemy's point of view; (3) **cover and concealment** from enemy fire and observation; and (4) natural and man-made **obstacles** that he must avoid.

All of these considerations help him select the best **avenue of approach,** a route from the line of departure to the objective that offers cover and concealment and best aids the movement and control of his unit.

Completing the Plan

The final plan of attack has two main parts—maneuver and fire support. The **maneuver plan** includes selection of routes of advance, assault position, platoon formation and order of march, and plans for seizing critical terrain, deployment for the assault, **and** reorganization on the objective.

The **fire support plan** includes **definite missions, position areas,** and **targets for all weapons** from the beginning through all phases of the attack.

Issuing the Order

From notes made during reconnaissance and planning, the platoon leader issues his attack order to his subordinate leaders at or near his OP. He tells them all he knows about the terrain. He requires them to take notes and questions each one to make sure every man understands the order and the plan of attack. A complete platoon attack order can be found in Appendix I.

Outline of Attack Order

Although given orally, the platoon attack order follows the outline of the standard operation order, which is:

1. Situation

    a. Information of the enemy.

    b. Information of friendly troops, to include the next higher unit's objective, missions and location of adjacent units, and fire support at hand from higher units.

2. Mission

    A short, clear statement of the platoon's mission.

3. Execution

    Explanation of each squad's mission, including: (1) instructions for deployment at the assault position; (2) security measures; (3) actions to overcome enemy resistance short of the objective; (4) instructions for reorganization on the objective; and (5) coordinating details, such as LD, time of attack, formation, order of march, route, and tentative assault position.

4. Administration and Logistics

    Location of battalion aid station. Instructions on how much ammunition will be carried and how it will be resupplied.

5. Command and Signal

    Prearranged signals; location of platoon leader and company commander.

Supervising

During the attack the platoon leader goes wherever he can best observe developments and control the action of his platoon. He sees that his plans are carried out and is alert to any need for a change in plans. He is particularly alert to enemy fire and disclosure of the main enemy position. He makes the greatest possible use of his subordinate leaders in this supervision.

PLATOON LEADER'S CHECKLIST FOR PLANNING THE ATTACK

1. Do you completely understand the company mission and plan of attack? .... ____

2. Do you understand the exact part your platoon is expected to play in it? .... ____

3. Have you made a map study and planned your reconnaissance? .... ____

4. Have you considered **every** course of action by which your platoon can accomplish its mission? .... ____

5. Have you checked each course of action against the enemy's capabilities for interfering with it? .... ____

6. Before going on reconnaissance, have you made arrangements for the movement of your platoon, if necessary, or sent final instructions as to what the men should do to prepare for the attack? .... ____

7. In planning your reconnaissance, have you allowed time to issue your order and for your squad leaders to reconnoiter, plan, and issue their orders? .... ____

8. Have you sent a messenger back with instructions as to where the squad leaders are to meet you to hear your attack order? .... ____

9. Have you arranged to coordinate your plans with—
    a. Unit leaders on right and left? .... ____
    b. Weapons platoon leader? .... ____
    c. Company commander? .... ____

10. While on reconnaissance, have you—
    a. Picked out the critical terrain features? ____
    b. Checked for observation and fields of fire? .... ____
    c. Looked for cover and concealment? .... ____
    d. Considered the natural and man-made obstacles? .... ____
    e. Picked out **the best** avenue of approach from the LD to the objective? .... ____

11. Have you, while on reconnaissance, noticed anything that makes it necessary for you to change your original plan of attack? .. ____

12. Have you selected the **one** plan that promises the best chance of success? .... ____

13. Does your plan provide these guides for maneuver:
    a. Routes of advance? .... ____
    b. Assault position? .... ____
    c. Platoon formation? .... ____
    d. Order of march within the formation? ____
    e. Plans for seizing critical terrain? .... ____
    f. Deployment for the assault? .... ____
    g. Reorganization on the objective? ...... ____

14. Does your plan include **detailed** provisions for fire support, giving instructions to every weapon from start to finish, covering—
    a. Definite missions? .... ____
    b. Position areas? .... ____
    c. Targets? .... ____
    d. When to lift or shift fires? .... ____

15. Does your plan fit in with the company plan and include all the necessary details from the company order? .... ____

16. Having selected a plan of action, have you decided just **who** is going to do **what?** And **when, where,** and **how** they will do it? Can you tell each unit **why** it is to do what you order? .... ____

17. Have you made complete notes so you can give your attack order clearly and completely? ____

18. Does your order include all the necessary elements of the standard operation order? ... ____

19. Have you acquainted your subordinate leaders thoroughly with the terrain? .... ____

20. Have you questioned each unit leader to see if he understands exactly what he is to do? ____

21. Does every unit leader know and understand the prearranged signals? .... ____

CHAPTER 5
THE PLATOON IN ATTACK

Action in the Assembly Area

While platoon and squad leaders are planning the attack, the rest of the men remain in the platoon assembly area. Here the men stack equipment not needed for the attack, receive combat loads of ammunition, extra or special equipment, and rations. Weapons squads, attached for the attack, join the platoon. Squad leaders issue orders to their squads. Men are allowed to get as much rest as possible.

Movement to the Attack Position

The assistant platoon sergeant usually moves the platoon to the attack position under control of the company executive officer. The move is made with the greatest possible secrecy.

The attack position is the last covered position occupied before crossing the line of departure. Platoons take up their formations here for crossing the line of departure and position themselves to cross immediately upon command or at a specified time. As little time as possible is spent here.

Crossing the Line of Departure

The line of departure (LD) is an imaginary line on the ground, usually along some prominent terrain feature that lies crosswise to the direction of attack. It can be a road, a ridge, the edge of a woods, or any other feature that is easily recognized.

Its purpose is to get the attacking units started off together so that they will hit the enemy in the right order and at the right time.

Moving Toward the Assault Position

The platoon moves toward the assault position quickly and aggressively. It makes the best possible use of cover, concealment, supporting fires, and smoke. It avoids bunching up and changes formation to fit the terrain and action.

If it receives enemy mortar or artillery fire, it moves quickly through or around the impact area. To stop or slow down is fatal.

Action Under Small-Arms Fire

If enemy small-arms fire becomes effective, the platoon leader returns the fire with his own and attached weapons. The 57-mm rifle and the 3.5-inch rocket launcher are particularly effective against enemy crew-served weapons. Any squad may also return enemy fire.

The platoon leader may have to request fire from outside the platoon. His main concern is to gain fire superiority by accurate and intense fire.

Fire and Maneuver

If the platoon leader cannot knock out the enemy resistance by fire, he uses fire and maneuver. Placing as much fire as possible on the enemy from the front, he maneuvers one or more squads—using the best cover and concealment possible—against the enemy from a different direction.

Surprise flanking fire from this maneuvering force alone may cause the enemy to withdraw. Or, it may make him shift to meet the new threat, allowing the original attacking force to move again.

The Assault Position

The assault position is as close to the enemy as friendly supporting fires permit. Although it is pointed out in the attack order, its exact location cannot be determined until the platoon nears the enemy position.

It should be less than 150 yards from the objective, be easily recognized on the ground, and afford some cover for deployment. The platoon takes up the platoon line formation as it approaches the position.

Beginning the Assault

The last 100 yards is pay dirt!

More attacks bog down between the assault position and the objective than anywhere else. The greatest hazard at this time is not the enemy, but confusion and loss of fire superiority.

The platoon leader names a base squad for direction and control. He usually moves behind it. He can start the assault when ready or on order of the company commander. In any event, he notifies him by radio or signal.

Shifting Supporting Fires

Only fires that are dangerous to the assaulting troops—such as mortar or artillery—shift as the assault begins. The company commander decides when to shift fires from direct-fire weapons. He bases his decision on observation and reports from platoon and fire-support unit leaders. A direct-fire gunner can shift his fire when he sees that it is falling too close to assaulting troops.

While this fire is being shifted, the platoon presses on and opens its own assault fire.

Assault Fire

The platoon moves toward the objective at a rapid walk, delivering assault fire as it goes. The fire must have volume and accuracy. It should hit the enemy as soon as possible after supporting fires shift.

The platoon leader uses his own and attached weapons to the limit. The 57-mm rifle, the 3.5-inch rocket launcher, light machine guns, and flame throwers should be used to fatten the fires of the weapons in the rifle squads.

The assault is pressed through the objective to its far edge.

Reorganization and Consolidation on the Objective

Immediately upon taking the objective, the platoon prepares to beat off enemy counterattack. The squads organize the sectors assigned in the platoon attack order. All crew-served weapons are brought up quickly and placed to cover possible routes of enemy counterattack.

The platoon leader inspects his platoon and improves the position. He replaces lost key men, redistributes ammunition, and gives his situation, strength, and ammunition reports to the company commander.

The Rifle Platoon as Reserve

A rifle platoon may be given a reserve mission. In this case, the platoon leader goes where he can observe the attacking units. He keeps in constant contact with the company commander so that he can receive orders without delay. He tries to think ahead of situations that may require his platoon to be used; he plans accordingly. His platoon advances by bounds at a specified distance behind the attack, ready for immediate use.

PLATOON LEADER'S CHECKLIST FOR THE ATTACK

1. Before leaving the assembly area, have you checked to see if your men have received—
    a. Combat loads of ammunition? .... ___
    b. Extra or special equipment? .... ___
    c. Rations? .... ___

2. Have you made arrangements for your squads to take up the prescribed formation quickly as they reach the attact position, so they can cross the LD on time and in the right order? ___

3. While moving toward the assault position, are your squads—
    a. Moving swiftly and aggressively? .... ___
    b. Taking full advantage of cover, concealment, supporting fires, and smoke? ...... ___
    c. Moving in such a way that **you** have control over them? .... ___

4. Are your crew-served weapons occupying positions where they can support your advance? ___

5. If enemy mortar or artillery fire begins to land in your zone, are you prepared to race through or around the impact area—and still maintain control? .... ___

6. To knock out enemy small-arms resistance short of the assault position, have you used every weapon available to you, including supporting fire from the company commander? .. ___

7. In preparing for fire and maneuver have you—

    a. Built up a strong base of fire to pin the enemy down? .... ____

    b. Checked to see that your squad leaders are giving proper fire orders and delivering accurate squad fire **on the enemy?** .... ____

    c. Given your maneuvering squad clear and complete instructions as to where it is to go and what it is to do? .... ____

    d. Made plans to reorganize and continue forward movement after resistance is knocked out? .... ____

8. As you approach the assault position, are your squads taking up the proper platoon line formation? .... ____

9. Are you still in control of the platoon? .... ____

10. Are your squads alined on the base squad? ____

11. Have you notified the company commander that you are ready to assault? .... ____

12. Are your weapons, organic and attached, all ready to open fire on the objective as you begin the assault so that you won't lose fire superiority as supporting fires shift? .... ____

13. As you move into the assault, are your men firing a heavy volume of **aimed** shots? ... ____

14. Are your crew-served weapons alert to knock out targets of opportunity, such as enemy machine guns, tanks, and other positions? .... ____

15. Have you cleared the objective to its far edge? .... ___

16. Are your squads reorganizing quickly on the objective as directed by you in the attack order? .... ___

17. Are your squads providing for local security? .... ___

18. Are your crew-served weapons taking positions with good fields of fire? .... ___

19. Is there any way you can improve your platoon's position in preparation for enemy counterattack? .... ___

20. Have you—
    a. Replaced lost key men? .... ___
    b. Redistributed ammunition? .... ___
    c. Prepared a report for the company commander on your situation, strength, and ammunition supply? .... ___

CHAPTER 6

THE RIFLE SQUAD IN ATTACK

The rifle squad leader follows about the same troop leading steps as his platoon leader. His reconnaissance is usually limited to observation from an OP. He studies the terrain and plans his attack, deciding what formations he will use. He looks the ground over for cover, concealment, and good avenues of approach in his zone.

> PRETTY OPEN COUNTRY
> ...ST OF THE WAY.
> ...OD SPOT ON THAT KNOLL
> ...R ENEMY OUTPOST.

Plan of Attack

The squad leader's plan of attack covers action from the crossing of the LD through reorganization on the objective. He plans in detail for action he thinks might take place, such as the need to take critical terrain or knock out enemy resistance short of the objective, and the need, if any, to change formation. He thinks constantly in terms of what **each** of his men will have to do.

Squad Attack Order

The squad leader gives his attack order from notes to his whole squad, usually in the assembly area. He sketches a rough map on the ground or a piece of paper to help tell his men about the terrain and action. His order includes detailed instructions for every man. He questions each man to make sure he understands the plan of attack and exactly what he is supposed to do.

His order follows the same outline given for the platoon leader on page 42. A sample squad attack order is given in Appendix II.

Crossing the Line of Departure

The squad moves from the assembly area to the attack position under platoon control. Once there, it takes up the formation it will use to cross the LD. The squad crosses the LD, usually in diamond formation, on signal from the platoon leader.

Moving Toward the Assault Position

While the squad is moving forward, the squad leader goes where he can best control his men. He keeps them moving forward at a steady, aggressive pace and makes sure that contact is maintained with units on his right and left and with his platoon leader.

Action Under Mortar and Artillery Fire

If mortar or artillery fire falls in the squad zone, the squad leader rushes his men quickly through or around the impact area. He uses prompt and forceful measures to see that his men don't scatter, hit the ground, or become panicky. An aggressive act by him, such as shouting directions and leading the rush through or around the area, will do much toward keeping his men moving forward together.

Action Under Small-Arms Fire

If enemy small-arms fire becomes effective before the assault position is reached, the squad leader has several things to do in a hurry. He must (1) gain fire superiority; (2) size up the situation; (3) decide what to do; (4) give orders and see that they are carried out. To gain fire superiority, he immediately deploys his squad and returns the fire, making sure that all of his fire power is being used—rifles, automatic rifles, hand and rifle grenades, his sniper—and that the fire is being aimed at likely enemy positions.

Sizing up the Situation

In sizing up the situation, the squad leader (1) estimates the enemy's size and location; (2) decides if the enemy can be knocked out by fire or if he will have to use fire and maneuver; and (3) determines if the position can be by-passed. These points lead him to a course of action. He issues fragmentary orders and follows his orders with close personal supervision.

Fire and Maneuver

In some instances, fire and maneuver is used within the squad. The squad leader has one part of his squad increase its rate of fire while two or three men, named by him, in another part of the squad, rush to a new firing position. These men then take up the fire and the squad leader names other men to advance. The automatic rifles are particularly useful in covering these rushes.

Action at the Assault Position

The squad begins to spread out as skirmishers when approaching the assault position. The squad leader checks the formation for dispersion, control, and position of the automatic riflemen. He tells the platoon leader when he is ready to assault. The men fix bayonets and take up aimed fire on the objective.

Riflemen in the Assault

On the platoon leader's signal, the squad moves to the far edge of the objective at a rapid walk, delivering assault fire as it goes. Each rifleman fires an **aimed** shot **from the shoulder** every two or three steps. They fire at any point on the ground that might conceal an enemy, such as clumps of bushes or folds in the ground. Hand and rifle grenades are very effective to blind or kill the enemy. The sniper is alert for shots at enemy key men, pillbox openings, and enemy weapons crews.

Automatic Riflemen in the Assault

The automatic riflemen carry their weapons slung from the shoulder and fire from the hip in short bursts, covering the entire squad front.

Squad Leaders in the Assault

The squad leader and assistant squad leader don't usually fire during the assault. They move close in rear of the line where they can shift about rapidly to keep up the fire, hold the squad alined on the base man, and press the men forward. They also keep alinement with the platoon's base squad.

Action on the Objective

When the objective is taken, the squad moves quickly to its assigned sector and gets ready to meet enemy counterattack. **The squad leader assigns each man a position and sector of fire.** He locates his automatic riflemen where they can cover all or a big part of the squad sector. He directs the sniper to a position with good fields of fire so that he can kill enemy key men trying to lead a counterattack.

Reorganization

The squad leader checks each man to determine casualties, condition of weapons, and amount of ammunition left. He replaces key men who have been killed or wounded, redistributes ammunition, and reports his losses and needs for weapons and ammunition to his platoon leader.

The Rifle Squad as Reserve

The platoon leader may designate a reserve squad (or squads). The reserve squad advances according to plan or on the platoon leader's order. The squad leader makes plans for any possible use of his squad that seems likely. Some missions he may be given are to protect an open flank, to attack from a new direction, or to take over the mission of another squad.

SQUAD LEADER'S CHECKLIST FOR THE ATTACK

1. Have you made a thorough terrain study, either—
    a. On the ground? .... ____
    b. On a map? .... ____

2. Have you, during this study, picked out good cover, concealment, and routes of approach? .... ____

3. In forming your plan, have you—
    a. Decided what formation you will use? .. ____
    b. Considered what possible enemy action may take place between the LD and the assault position? .... ____
    c. Decided what **each man** in the squad—especially the automatic riflemen—will do? ____

4. Before giving your order to your men, did you tell them all you know about the terrain in your zone? .... ____

5. Does your order include all the necessary details and follow the sequence of the standard operation order? .... ____

6. Have you questioned each man to make sure he understands the plan of attack and just what he is to do? .... ____

7. In the attack position, have you checked the formation of your squad? .... ____

8. Is the formation the right one for the terrain and situation while crossing the LD and moving to the assault position? .... ____

9. Have you watched your platoon leader for his signal to cross the LD? .... ____

10. As you move toward the assault position, is your squad spread out and yet completely under your control? .... ____

11. Are you in contact with—
 a. Units on your right and left? .... ____
 b. Your platoon leader? .... ____

12. Is your squad moving as rapidly as possible and making the best use of cover and concealment? .... ____

13. If you come under enemy mortar or artillery fire, are you prepared to take aggressive action to lead your men through or around the impact area—and still be in control? .... ____

14. When enemy small-arms fire becomes effective short of the objective, does your squad return the fire? .... ____

15. Have you issued a fire order? .... ____

16. Is your squad's fire **hitting** the probable enemy position? .... ____

17. Have you picked good positions and pointed out sectors of fire for your two automatic riflemen? .... ____

18. Have you notified your platoon leader of the situation? .... ____

19. Have you asked him for additional fire support, if needed? .... ____

20. If you plan to advance by fire and maneuver, are you in position to direct part of the squad forward and keep the rest of the men firing accurately? .... ____

21. Are you taking up the "as skirmishers" formation as you reach the assault position? .. ____

22. Are your men well spread out and generally in line with the base man? .... ____

23. Is your squad alined with the platoon's base squad? .... ____

24. Are you in contact with your platoon leader, alert for his signal to begin the assault? ____

25. Are your automatic riflemen in line where they can cover the whole squad front as they move? .... ____

26. Have your riflemen fixed bayonets? ..... ____

27. Have you told your platoon leader that you are ready to begin the assault? .... ____

28. As you move out in the assault, are you and your assistant squad leader in a position where you can watch and control the men? .... ____

29. Are your men firing fast enough and taking aimed shots at enemy or spots on the ground likely to conceal an enemy? .... ____

30. Are you watching for targets of opportunity and correcting your men's fire, if wild or inaccurate? .... ____

31. After you cross the objective to its far edge, have you assigned each man a position and sector of fire? .... ____

32. Are your automatic riflemen and sniper in position with good fields of fire, covering the most likely approaches for enemy counterattack? .... ____

33. After your men are in position, have you—

    a. Checked for casualties? .... ____

    b. Checked the condition of weapons? .... ____

    c. Checked your supply of ammunition? .. ____

    d. Replaced lost key men? .... ____

    e. Collected ammunition from casualties and redistributed it? .... ____

    f. Reported your situation, strength, and ammunition needs to your platoon leader? ____

CHAPTER 7

THE WEAPONS SQUAD IN THE ATTACK

The weapons squad furnishes close-in fire support for the rifle platoon. The platoon leader directs how the two machine guns will be used at the start of the attack, selecting one of these three general uses:

1. Have both teams fire from positions near the LD.
2. Have one team fire from the LD and send the other with the platoon.
3. Send both teams with the platoon.

Firing Positions

His selection is influenced chiefly by the location of suitable firing positions. Here are the marks of a good firing position:
 1. Good observation over target or sector of fire.
 2. Good observation of the maneuvering squads.
 3. Good fields of fire.
 4. Good cover and concealment.
 5. Presence of covered routes to the position for movement to it and for resupply of ammunition.

Troop Leading Steps

The weapons squad leader follows the same troop-leading steps as the rifle squad leader. During his reconnaissance he looks especially for exact weapons positions, routes to these positions, and routes for movement forward during the attack. He decides **in detail** how the guns will be used, basing his plans on general instructions from his platoon leader.

Weapons Squad Attack Order

The squad leader's attack order follows the standard operation order. But in paragraph 3 he emphasizes these things:
1. Mission of **each** machine-gun team.
2. First firing position (or unit to be followed).
3. First targets or sectors of fire.
4. Time of opening fire.
5. Action as attack progresses.
6. Use of machine guns during the assault.
7. Plans for moving guns forward.
8. Action during reorganization.

Control

When both machine guns are used in the same fire mission, the squad leader controls them. When they fire separate missions, the squad leader controls one team and the team leader (gunner) controls the other. The squad or team leader adjusts fire and uses the ammunition bearers to keep the guns supplied.

Conduct of Fire

The machine-gun squad or teams are given a definite target or sector of fire. The squad leader points out the target, directs the method and rate of fire, and gives the signal for opening fire. He watches the movement of the rifle squads and plans ahead so he can hand-carry his guns forward to keep up his close fire support. When firing as a squad, one team usually displaces first, while the other continues to fire.

Ammunition

If possible, ammunition is hauled to the attack position by vehicle. The ammunition bearers keep up the supply by hand carry during the attack. If they cannot keep up the supply, the squad leader asks his platoon leader for more men to help.

Assault and Reorganization

If good positions can be found, both guns are placed to fire in close support of the rifle squads during the assault. If not, they will be carried and fired from the hip.

The weapons squad joins the rifle squads quickly on the objective. The guns are placed to cover the most likely approaches for enemy counterattack.

APPENDIX I

SAMPLE PLATOON LEADER'S ORDER

"You've had a look at the terrain. Here's the order. Take notes.

"1. Aggressor holds HILLS 2 and 7. Three Aggressors have been observed moving around RIDGE 6. Co. 'C' reports small-arms fire from estimated 2 riflemen on HIRAM HILL.

"The company continues the attack to the southeast at 0900 hours in a column of platoons, 3d Plat leading, followed by the 2d Plat and the 1st Plat with the mission of seizing HILL 7. Co 'B,' on left, seizes HILL 2. 3d Bn, 7th Inf occupies RASMUSSEN HILL and will hold in place until HILL 7 is secure. 81-mm mortar fire available on call.

"2. Our platoon, with the 3d 57-mm Squad attached, attacks to seize RIDGE 6 and will be prepared to continue the attack on order to the left half of HILL 7.

"3. We'll cross the LD in platoon column and move all the way to the assault position that way unless something happens to make us change formation. We'll take up the platoon line as we approach the assault position.

"a. Sgt Haley, your first squad will lead. Move over that finger, stay this side of the erosion ditch and clear HIRAM HILL. Hold up on HIRAM HILL, stay off the sky line, until the platoon crosses the saddle to the left and abreast of your position, then displace over the top of HIRAM HILL to the assault position as the right squad in the platoon line. Take the part of the objective that is right of the tall, right pine tree. Reorganize from two to four o'clock.

"b. Sgt Taylor, have your 2d Squad follow the RL Team in column. When Sgt Haley's 1st Squad has cleared HIRAM HILL, move on my signal to the saddle between HUMP HILL and HIRAM HILL. Move rapidly on order to assault position as center and base squad. Your portion of the objective during the assault is from the right, tall pine tree to a point 20 yards left of the left, tall pine. Reorganize from 12 to 2 o'clock.

"c. Sgt Schultz, your 3d Squad will follow the 2d Squad to the assault position. Deploy your squad 'as skirmishers' to the left of the 2d Squad before you reach the assault position. You take the left part of the objective from 20 yards left of the left pine tree over across HUNTER'S TRAIL. Get some men across the trail at the assault position. Reorganize from 10 to 12 o'clock.

"d. Sgt Sawyer, your weapons squad will position itself initially on HUMP HILL near the RIGHT DRAW to support the 1st Squad to HIRAM HILL. Displace the squad when fires are masked. Displace 1st Team to HIRAM HILL to continue support during attack to RIDGE 6. Keep an eye on the WOODS X area for targets. This team will displace to RIDGE 6 when fire is masked during the assault and will reorganize in the 1st Squad sector. The 2d Team will displace forward from initial positions when fire is masked to that finger on HUMP HILL. Support attack to RIDGE 6. Watch for targets in the low ground between HILL 4 and RIDGE 6 and the draw leading up from WOODS X to the assault position between HIRAM HILL and RIDGE 6. When fire is masked, displace team forward and reorganize in the 2d Squad sector. You control the 2d Team and I will have the ass't plat sgt control the 1st Team.

"e. Sgt Ropp, your RL team will follow the 1st Squad in column until the 1st Squad moves out for HIRAM HILL, then go into position on that finger to the right front. After HIRAM HILL is secured, move to the assault position behind the 2d Squad. Follow the 2d Squad in the assault by 50 yards. Take up positions during reorganization on the objective near the road at 12 o'clock.

"f. Sgt Kimel, initially put your 57-mm rifle in position on HUMP HILL near the RIGHT DRAW. Be able to support the 1st Squad to HIRAM HILL. Displace forward when your fire is masked. When HIRAM HILL is secure, go into position on the hill to support the attack on to RIDGE 6. Watch right flank, the WOODS X area, for targets. As your fire is masked by the assault, displace to RIDGE 6. Reorganize in the 2d Squad sector in positions where fire can be delivered on HILL 7 and the WOODS X area.

"4. Ammunition is on carrier vicinity of the company CP. Battalion aid station unchanged.

"5. Company CP, no change. Plat Sgt Rundell, move near the head of the 2d Squad. Keep me under observation at all times. Control the left flank of the platoon line during the assault. Watch me for signals. Ass't Plat Sgt Kite will control the base of fire until fires are masked. He will take the 1st MG Team and the 57-mm Rifle to HIRAM HILL. After positioning these weapons Sgt Kite will move the 1st Squad to the assault position and control the right flank squad in the platoon line during the assault. Emergency signal to lift indirect supporting fires is a green smoke streamer. Initially I will follow the 1st Squad. During the assault I'll be behind the 2d (base) Squad in the center. Time is 0600."

APPENDIX II
SAMPLE SQUAD LEADER'S ORDER

"All right fellows, gather around where you can see this sketch I've drawn on the ground. This is the area we're going to attack over. This is ABLE HILL and BAKER HILL where the 2d Bn is holding now. Here is HILL 206, the SPUR and HILL 234 on to the North. A stream runs down through here with a swampy area or pond here. There's an improved road here, in the 2d Platoon's zone on our left, and a highway here, about 500 yards to the front with a knocked-out bridge here. Woods run from here on up to the front, right to the base of HILL 206. Get the picture? How about it Smothers? Jones? Kovac?

"1. The enemy is defending HILL 206, the SPUR, and HILL 234, with an estimated reinforced rifle platoon.

"Our platoon attacks to seize HILL 206 and be prepared to continue the attack to HILL 234. We'll pass through elements of 2d Bn which are holding ABLE HILL. The 2d Platoon will be on our left to take the SPUR. Company 'D' MG's and 81's, 1st Plat 4.2's and the direct support artillery battalion start preparation fires at H-5.

"2. Our squad seizes the right portion of the platoon objective.

"3. The line of departure is the road along the ridge. Our route is to the left of the POND and the KNOLL. The assault position is there at the edge of the woods. From the LD to the assault position we are the lead squad in a platoon-column formation. For the assault we are the right squad of a platoon line. Time of attack is 0900 hours.

"We'll cross the line of departure, where the pole line crosses the road, in squad column. We'll probably stay in squad column all the way to the assault position and then deploy as skirmishers for the assault.

"Each of you knows his position in the squad. Jones and Brown, keep well out to the front for security. Kovac, be ready to lob grenades with your launcher and adaptors. You AR men get into the fight quick if we hit any resistance and Smothers, watch me for instructions. On the objective our squad reorganizes from 1-3. Let's go get 'em, and everyone watch me for signals.

"4. That's the aid station up the road on the left there and the company ammo supply point will set up in rear of BAKER HILL.

"5. The emergency signal for lifting supporting fires is a green smoke streamer. The company CP will remain here. Lt Hurst will follow our squad. I'll be near the front of the formation. Time is 0730.

"Any questions? No? Well, let me ask some, then. Kovac, what do you do when ...."

INDEX

A

Action:
  In assembly area, 47
  On the objective, 75
  Under mortar and artillery fire, 67
  To overcome resistance, 42
  Under small-arms fire, 51
Administration and logistics, 42
Ammunition in attack, 42, 88
Arranging coordination, 38
As skirmishers, 27
Assault and reorganization, 89
Assault:
  Automatic riflemen in, 73
  Beginning the, 54
  Fire, 56
  Position, 42, 53, 66, 71, 89
  Riflemen in, 72
  Shifting supporting fires in, 55
  Squad leaders in, 74
Attack:
  Check list, 44-46, 58-61, 78-81
  In general, 7
  Order, company, 34
  Outline of platoon order, 42
  Platoon in, 47
  Preparing platoon for, 33
  Rifle squad in:
    Action at assault position, 71
    Action on the objective, 75
    Action under mortar and artillery fire, 67
    Action under small-arms fire, 68
    Automatic riflemen in assault, 73
    Crossing line of departure, 65
    Moving toward assault position, 66
    Order, 64
    Plan of attack, 63
    Reorganization, 76
    Riflemen in assault, 72
    Sizing up the situation, 68, 69
    Squad leaders in, 74
    Weapons squad in, 82
  Automatic riflemen in assault, 73
Avenue of approach, 39

B

Battalion aid station, 42
Beginning planning, 36
Beginning the assault, 54

C

Check list for:
  Platoon leader in attack, 58-61
  Platoon leader planning attack, 44-46
  Squad leader in attack, 78-81
Column, platoon, 28
Column, squad, 25
Combat formations:
  Essentials of, 24
  General, 23
Command and signal, 42
Company attack order, 34
Completing the plan of attack, 40
Control, 24, 28, 86
Cover and concealment, 39, 83
Critical terrain features, 39
Crossing line of departure, 65

D

Definite missions, 40
Diamond, squad, 26

E

Echelon, platoon, 30
Essentials of combat formations, 24
Execution, 42

F

Fields of fire, 39, 83
Fighting 'em, 14
Finding 'em, 12
Finishing 'em, 15
Fire and maneuver:
  Infantry tactics, 8
  Platoon, 52
  Squad, 70
Fire support plan, 40
Fire superiority, 9
Firing positions, 83
Fixing 'em, 13
Flame throwers, 56
Flexibility, 24
Form for attack order, 42
Formations:
  Attack, 42
  Platoon:
    Platoon column, 28
    Platoon echelon, 30
    Platoon line, 32
    Platoon vee, 31
    Platoon wedge, 29
  Squad:
    As skirmishers, 27
    Squad column, 25
    Squad diamond, 26

G

Getting ready to attack, 33
Going on reconnaissance, 39

I

Infantry's job, 8
Infantry tactics, 8
Information:
  Of enemy, 42
  Of friendly troops, 42
Issuing the order, 41

L

Last 100 yards, 54
Line of departure, crossing in attack:
  Coordination in order, 42
  Platoon, 49
  Squad, 65
Line, platoon, 32

M

Making arrangements, 37
Maneuver plan, 40
Maneuvering force, 11
Mission, 42, 85
Movement to attack position, platoon, 48

O

Observation points, 39
Obstacles, 39
Operation order, standard, 42
Order:
  Platoon attack, outline of, 42
  Rifle squad attack, 64
  Sample:
    Platoon leader's, 90-93
    Squad leader's, 94-95
  Weapons squad attack, 85
Organization:
  For fire support, 10
  Platoon, 17, 19
  Rifle squad, 17, 18
  Weapons squad, 22
Outline of platoon attack order, 42

P

Plan of attack, rifle squad, 63
Platoon:
  Attack position, 48, 50
  Action in assembly area, 47

Check lists, 44-46, 58-61
Crossing line of departure, 49
Formations:
  Platoon column, 28
  Platoon echelon, 30
  Platoon line, 32
  Platoon vee, 31
  Platoon wedge, 29
Headquarters, 20, 21
Organization, 19, 20
Preparing for attack, 33
Troop leading steps:
  Arranging coordination, 38
  Beginning planning, 36
  Completing the plan, 40
  Going on reconnaissance, 39
  Issuing the order, 41
  Making arrangements, 37
Position areas, 40
Prearranged signals, 42

R

Recoilless rifle, 56
Reorganization:
  On objective, 42
  Rifle squad, 76
  Weapons squad, 79
Reserve:
  Rifle platoon, 57
  Rifle squad, 77
Rifle squad:
  Attack order, 64
  Formations, 25, 26, 27
  In attack, 62, 81
  Organization, 17, 18
  Squad leader in assault, 74
Riflemen in assault, 72
Rocket launcher, 56

S

Sample orders:
  Platoon leader's, 90-93
  Squad leader's, 94-95
Sector of fire, 75
Security, 24
Security measures, 42
Situation, 42
Squad:
  Attack order, 64
  Formations:
    As skirmishers, 27
    Squad column, 25
    Squad diamond, 26
  Leaders in attack, 74
  Rifle, 18
  Weapons, 22
Shifting supporting fires, 55
Sizing up the situation, 68, 69
Supervising platoon attack, 43

T

Targets for weapons, 40
Time of attack, 42
Triangular infantry organization, 16
Troop leading steps:
  Platoon leader, 35
  Rifle squad leader, 62
  Weapons squad leader, 84

V

Vee, platoon, 31

W

Weapons squad:
  In attack:
    Ammunition, 88
    Assault and reorganization, 89
    Conduct of fire, 87
    Control of, 86
    Firing positions, 83
    Order, 85
    Troop leading steps, 84
  Organization, 22
Wedge, platoon, 29